# Smelling and Tasting

## Paul Humphrey

Photography by Chris Fairclough

First published in 2007 by
Franklin Watts
338 Euston Road
London NW1 3BH

Franklin Watts Australia
Level 17/207 Kent Street
Sydney NSW 2000

© 2007 Franklin Watts

ISBN: 978 0 7496 7452 6 (hbk)
ISBN: 978 0 7496 7464 9 (pbk)

Dewey classification number: 612.8'7

A CIP catalogue record for this book is available
from the British Library.

Planning and production by Discovery Books Limited
Editor: Rachel Tisdale
Designer: Ian Winton
Photography: Chris Fairclough
Series advisors: Diana Bentley MA and Dee Reid MA,
Fellows of Oxford Brookes University

The author, packager and publisher would like to thank the following
people for their participation in this book: Auriel and Ottilie Austin-Baker, Bryn
Stallard-Pearson, Harriet and Imogen Stanley, Lucas Tisdale, the students and
teachers of Penn Hall School, Wolverhampton.

Printed in China

Franklin Watts is a division of Hachette Children's Books.

# Contents

Five senses 4

Smelling and tasting 6

Nice and nasty 8

Outdoor smells 10

Indoor smells 12

Sweet and salty 14

Bitter, sour and savoury 16

Spicy and cool 18

Fruity tastes 20

Dinner time! 22

Word bank 24

# Five senses

You have five senses. They are seeing, touching, hearing, smelling and tasting.

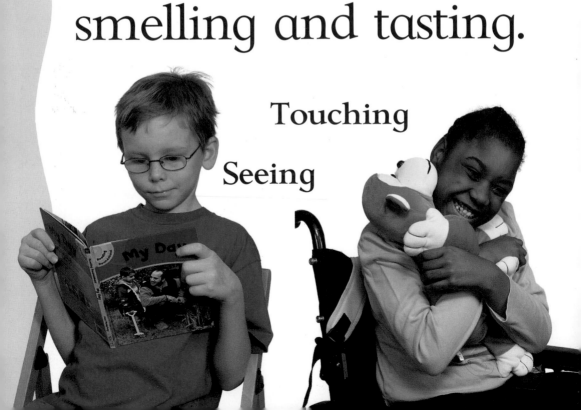

Touching

Seeing

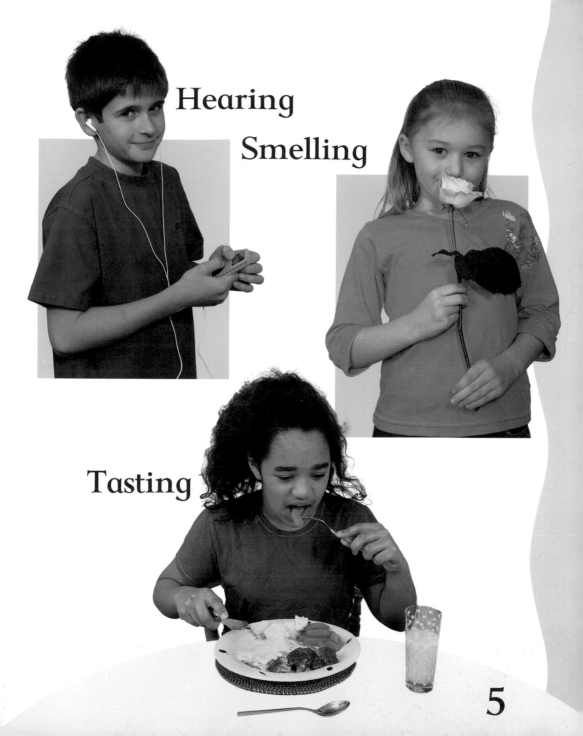

Hearing

Smelling

Tasting

5

# Smelling and tasting

You smell things with your nose.

You taste things
with your tongue.

# Nice and nasty

Some things
smell nice.

# Some things smell nasty.

# Outdoor smells

We like the smell of newly mown grass...

...and autumn leaves.

# Indoor smells

We can smell dinner cooking...

...and toast burning!

# Sweet and salty

Mangoes taste sweet.

Crisps taste
salty.

# Bitter, sour and savoury

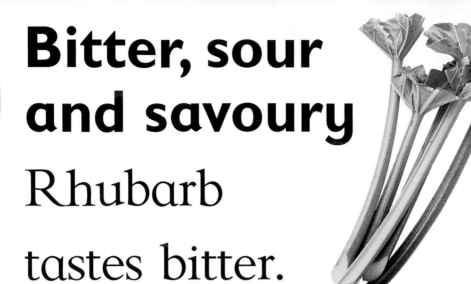

Rhubarb tastes bitter.

Lemons taste sour.

# Cheese has a savoury taste.

# Spicy and cool

Some things taste spicy and hot.

# Some things taste cool.

# Fruity tastes

Apples taste different to oranges...

...or strawberries.

# Dinner time!

Sometimes we like to smell things before we taste them.

What is your favourite smell and taste?

# Word bank

Look back for these words and pictures.

Bitter

Cool

Nasty smells

Nice smells

Nose

Salty

Savoury

Sour

Spicy

Sweet

Tongue